Sea Otters
Little Clowns of the Sea

Sea Otters
Little Clowns of the Sea

by **MARGARET DAVIDSON**

illustrated by **MERYL MEISLER**

SCHOLASTIC INC.
New York Toronto London Auckland Sydney Tokyo

ISBN 0-590-32720-8

Text copyright © 1984 by Margaret Davidson. Illustrations copyright © 1984 by Scholastic Inc. All rights reserved. Published by Scholastic Inc.

12 11 10 9 8 7 6 5 4 3 2 1   4   4 5 6 7 8/8

Printed in the U.S.A.   09

For good friends
Ruth and Bill Gross

Stand on a California cliff one day, or walk along a beach, and you may be lucky. You may see a group of southern sea otters not far from shore.

Some are sleeping, bobbing along on their backs. Some are busy eating shellfish snacks. But others are sure to be doing what sea otters seem to love most — playing otter games.

Two otters are "playing catch." Their "ball" is a big clam shell.

Two others are tugging on the ends of a long strand of seaweed. They pull and pull until — *pop!* — the seaweed rips in half.

And look! Over there some young otters are racing back and forth in a fast game of tag.

No wonder these furry animals are so often called "the clowns of the sea."

Sea otters look more like giant teddy bears than animals that live in the water. They have shiny black eyes and little pointed ears. Their front paws are tipped with catlike claws. Their bodies are wrapped in thick coats of fur. They even have tails.

But you can tell that otters are water animals by their big hind flippers. The flippers help the sea otter dive, roll, and somersault in the water — as gracefully as any circus acrobat.

Dolphins, whales, walruses, seals, and sea otters are all mammals that live in the sea. Mammals must breathe air. So no matter how deep or how far they swim underwater, these ocean-going creatures must sooner or later come up for a gulp of fresh air.

The sea otter is the smallest sea mammal of all.

WHALE

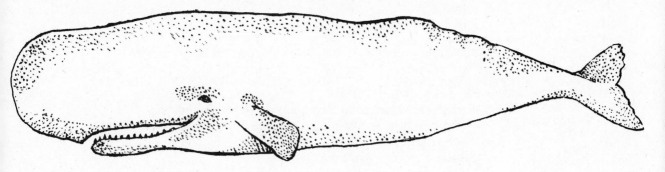

DOLPHINS

WALRUS

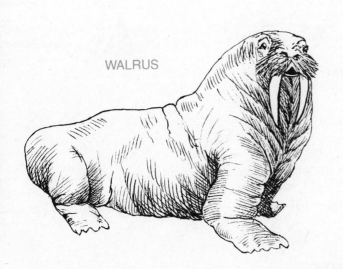

SEA OTTER

Sometimes when a sea otter spots something interesting in the distance, it raises itself partway out of the water, places a paw above its eyes, and tries to get a good look, just as a person might do.

Sea otters have sharp eyesight both above and under the water. They hear very well. And of all the sea mammals, they have the keenest sense of smell.

Most of the time the otter slowly paddles its hind flippers up and down and drifts from place to place on its back. This is every otter's favorite position.

It even sleeps on its back. (If it slept facedown, it would quickly drown.) On a cloudy or rainy day, the otter dozes with its paws tucked against its furry chest. On a sunny day it manages to sleep just as well — it simply shades its eyes with its paws.

But when a sea otter really wants to get somewhere, it rolls over onto its stomach and pumps its flippers hard. Even then, it doesn't go very fast. Whales and dolphins can swim faster than 20 miles an hour. Eight miles per hour is a sea otter's very top speed.

Southern sea otters live off the coast of central California. They don't travel to faraway places at all. Their lives are spent in a very small area called the *home range*.

Sea otters don't go very far from shore, either. They are almost always found in water no deeper than 50 to 100 feet.

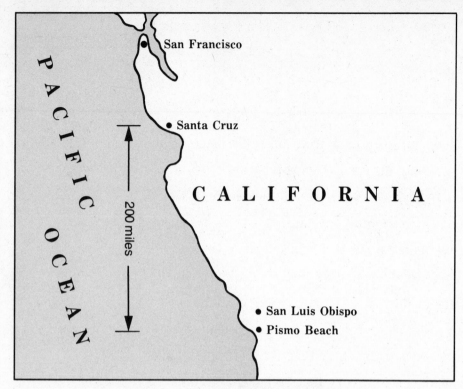

All California sea otters live near one another—within 200 miles.

Otters can live where the water is clear. But they seem to prefer living near a plant called *kelp*.

Kelp is a kind of giant seaweed that grows in the ocean. The kelp plants grow in bunches called beds and are rooted to the ocean floor, the way trees are rooted in the earth.

Thick stems rise up through the water like tree trunks through air. At the surface far above, long strands of brownish-green kelp spread out across the water like leafy tops of trees.

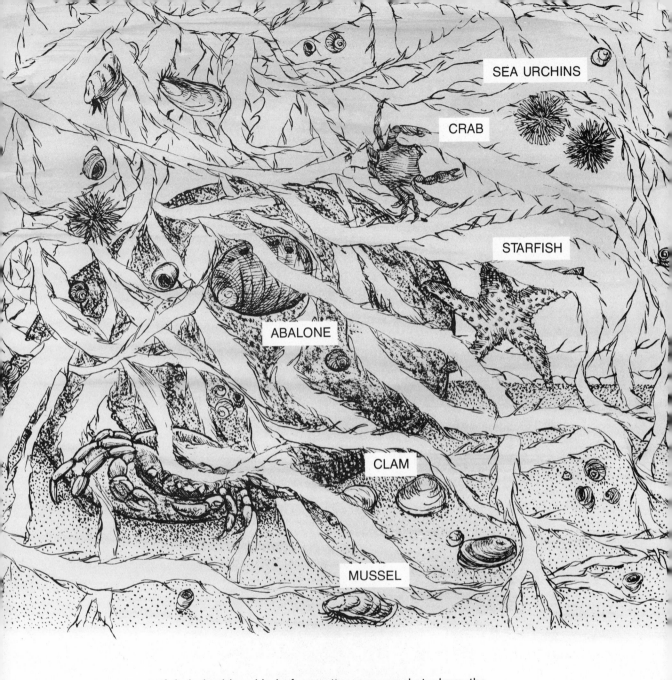

SEA URCHINS

CRAB

STARFISH

ABALONE

CLAM

MUSSEL

A kelp bed is a kind of sea otter supermarket where the otter can find lots of good things to eat. Otters eat small sea animals such as the ones shown here. Some experts say the otter eats at least 25 different kinds of creatures. Others say that 40 or so animals make up the sea otter's menu.

Finding Food

Sea otters don't eat the kelp plants — otters are not plant-eaters. But among the stems and roots of the kelp beds, sea otters find tasty sea creatures to eat — starfish, sea urchins, clams, mussels, and many others.

One thing a southern sea otter almost never eats is fish. Even when an otter swims as fast as it can, it can't catch a much faster fish zipping by.

When the water is still and the sky is bright, the sharp-eyed otter has very little trouble spotting its next meal — even on the ocean floor far below. But often storms churn up the water and fill it with clouds of mud and sand.

The otter doesn't go hungry, though. Even at night it can find food. It swims along, pat-pat-patting its paws on everything it passes. It can tell by touch when it comes across a familiar — and good-tasting — shape.

Sometimes the otter finds food with its whiskers, too. When something touches the otter's sensitive whiskers, they wriggle or vibrate just a little. From these tiny movements the otter knows whether it is touching a plant, a rock — or its next meal.

After it finds a snack, the otter comes back to the surface to eat. It never eats underwater. Sometimes the otter comes up with just one clam or squid or starfish in its paws. But more often it brings up a number of different good things at once.

How can the otter carry so much in one trip? A sea otter's furry coat is very loose. So before it dives for food it pushes a paw deep into the fur under its arm. This forms a kind of deep pocket or pouch. All sorts of good things can be stored in this fur-lined market basket.

A sea otter's teeth are big and rounded — just right for crushing the shells of small snails or crabs. But some shells are too hard and thick for even a sea otter's strong teeth to crush. The sea otter finds a way to open them just the same — with the help of a tool.

A sea otter's tool is a stone. It finds a good-sized flat rock on the ocean floor and tucks it into the pouch along with some food. Then up goes the otter, right to the top of the water.

It places the rock on its furry chest. It plucks out a clam or a mussel and pounds it down on the stone dinnerplate. *Rat-a-tat-tat!* It pounds until the shell shatters. Quickly the sea otter sucks out the soft insides — and spits out any leftover bits of shell.

When a sea otter smashes a clam on a stone, it is using a tool. People use tools. So do some of the great apes. The sea otter is the only other mammal we know of that makes things easier for itself this way.

Even with the help of the stone, a sea otter often has to work hard to get the goody inside. It can smash a sea urchin in nine or ten whacks. But a mussel often needs 35 blows or more to crack.

Sea otters also find another use for their tools. All otters love to eat the giant sea snail called *abalone*. But abalone are very well protected indeed. Their shells are especially hard and thick.

And that's not all. An abalone has a footlike muscle sticking out of its shell. This muscle acts like a powerful suction cup. When the abalone holds onto a big rock, it is almost impossible to pry it loose.

People like to eat abalone, too. When a human diver goes hunting for abalone, he usually takes a heavy, metal crowbar with him. Even then it may take a person many minutes to loosen the giant snail's stubborn grip.

The otter is not nearly as strong as a man with a crowbar. But it manages to get what it wants all the same. It pounds and pounds at the abalone with *its* special tool — a stone.

The otter bangs away until it chips a small hole in the abalone's shell. This probably doesn't hurt the abalone. But it does seem to stun it. Often the startled snail loosens its hold on the rock for a moment. Seconds later the sea otter is swimming up to the top with its hard-earned prize.

Sea otters spend a lot of time looking for food and then eating it. They need to eat so much because food helps keep them warm.

Sea otters, like all mammals, are warm-blooded. This means that their body temperature must remain the same no matter how hot or cold it is around them.

And any animal's body heat leaks away very quickly in water. Still, the otter manages to keep warm even when the sea is very cold. Its fur coat helps a great deal. But the food it eats is just as important. Food — lots and lots of it — is the fuel that keeps a sea otter warm.

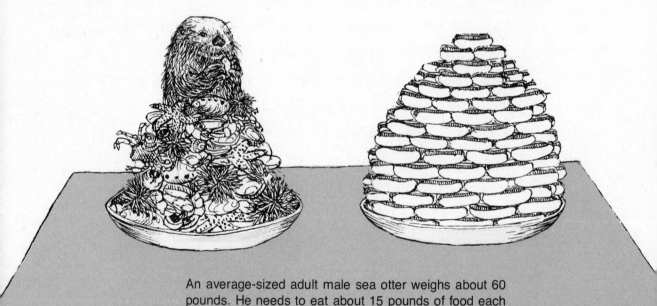

An average-sized adult male sea otter weighs about 60 pounds. He needs to eat about 15 pounds of food each day. A 60-pound child would have to eat 96 hot dogs — with or without mustard — to keep up with the little sea otter!

A Matter of Life and Death

Eating is hard work for an otter. So most otters take a nap after their meal. But before an otter can sleep, there is something it must do. It must waterproof itself.

A sea otter doesn't look like the other mammals of the sea. It is different in another very important way. A sea otter lives its whole life in the water — yet water must never touch its skin.

A walrus sits on a cake of ice for hours and never feels chilly at all. A giant blue whale swims in the freezing waters of the South Atlantic and doesn't get a bit cold, either. That's because walruses and whales and all the other mammals of the sea are protected by a thick layer of fat under their skins. This blubbery blanket keeps them warm in the coldest of seas.

But sea otters have no fatty layer under their skins. They have only their fine fur coats to keep them from quickly freezing to death.

Yet how can even the thickest fur keep out water for long? The sea otter solves this life-and-death problem by waterproofing its coat. This is called *grooming* — and it keeps the otter busy for many hours each day.

First the otter rubs and scrubs its coat, trying to squeeze out as much water as it can. Sometimes it twists and wrings its fur, just like a person wringing out a wet washcloth.

Then the otter combs its coat with its long, catlike claws.

It rolls over and over in the water, from side to side and head over heels. All this turning and twisting churns up air bubbles. Many bubbles are caught between the fine inner hairs of the otter's coat.

Afterwards, the otter slides its paws across the surface of its coat. This smooths the very top layer of hairs together into a kind of outer shell or skin — a skin to keep the air bubbles inside.

And still the sea otter isn't finished. Now it takes a deep breath . . . twists around . . . and blows *more* air into its fur. It puffs and puffs, just like someone blowing up a balloon, until millions of tiny air bubbles are trapped deep in its coat.

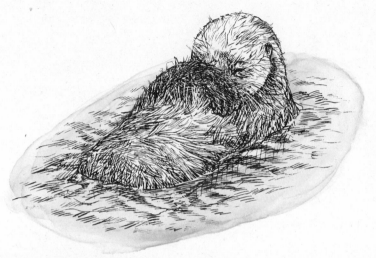

Sea otters always groom especially carefully after they eat. They must get rid of any leftover bits of shell or slimy chunks of food that may be caught in their coats. If they didn't, their fur would soon become soiled and matted. Then the cold water would quickly seep through. And as one scientist said, "A dirty otter is soon a dead otter."

Many times a day an otter whirls and twirls, pats and puffs and fluffs its coat. It will never have a nice thick layer of blubber like other sea mammals. But it will always be just as safe —wrapped in a toasty warm blanket of air.

The Good-Natured Sea Otter

An old male otter is taking a nap. Slowly, quietly, a young one swims up behind him. Suddenly the young otter leaps in the air — and comes plopping down smack in the middle of the sleeping otter's rounded belly. *Splash!* The poor otter sinks out of sight. What a way to wake up from a nap!

But the old otter doesn't seem to mind. He just swims a few feet away and falls asleep again.

Sea otters are very social animals. They spend a great deal of time swimming and sleeping and playing in groups called *rafts*.

Grown male otters almost always stay together in one
raft. Females and their young usually gather in another.

There's only one thing sea otters do alone — eat. Each otter seems to have a special part of the ocean it calls its own — a kind of private dining room. Other otters almost never bother an eating otter when it's in the middle of a meal. But every once in a while a hungry otter will sneak up and snatch away another otter's food.

What happens then? Nothing. The otter who has just lost a part of its dinner doesn't even snap or snarl. It just rolls over and dives down for something else to eat.

This doesn't surprise people who study otters. They know that sea otters are especially gentle and friendly animals. They simply do not like to fight.

People who have watched otters feel something else. They believe that sea otters are more than gentle and friendly. They believe that sea otters also seem to *care* about what happens to each other.

Once some scientists wanted to study sea otters up close. So they caught three — a big male and two smaller females — in a net. As soon as the otters were freed from the net, the big male threw himself over his two smaller companions. Every time the men came close he hissed fiercely. It was plain he thought he was protecting the other two otters from some terrible danger.

Another time long, long ago when people were allowed to hunt otters, a mother and her pup were sunning themselves on a rock. A hunter came along and killed the pup. Eight days later he returned — and the mother was still there. She was little more than skin and bones. She had not eaten a thing in all that time. A short while later she died of starvation. Or was it a broken heart?

Fun and Games

Almost all young animals love to play. But many animals forget this sense of fun as they grow older. Not sea otters. They are *always* ready to have a good time.

Otters of all ages ride the waves when the surf is high. They also play catch and tug-of-war and tag and hide-and-seek in the kelp beds.

When they play catch, their ball is usually an air-filled bulb of kelp. But if a kelp bulb isn't handy, they often find something else to throw. They have been seen many times tossing a shell back and forth. And once when someone threw an old hubcap into the water, several otters turned it into a ball at once.

Young otters especially enjoy rough-and-tumble games. They love to wrestle, rolling round and round in each other's arms. Sometimes they beat on each other with their fists and chew on each other's faces with their sharp baby teeth. But not too hard. They never seem to forget that this is just a game they are playing.

Feeling Happy, Feeling Sad

It's not easy to tell what some sea animals are feeling. They may be happy or sad or scared or mad, but they usually look and sound the same. Not sea otters. They show their feelings in many different ways. One is by the sounds they make.

Sea otters are not quiet animals. They chuckle, chortle, coo, whistle, wail, bawl, scream, snarl, growl, grunt, hiss, bark, and whine.

Scientists think they know what some of these sounds mean. Sea otters scream when they are frightened and growl when they are angry. If something strange startles them by coming too close they will hiss. "Stay away!" they are warning.

When otters don't get what they want quickly enough they often whine or whistle. A pup who is hungry or tired or just out of sorts bawls — *waah-waaah!* — just like a human baby.

Mother otters coo to their little ones. It's a way of showing love. And when sea otters are especially happy they chuckle. Often groups of sea otters float along together, making the same chuckling sound. One scientist called these chuckles "otter small talk."

Sea otters also "talk" with their bodies. When they are surprised or worried they hold out their paws — palms up — as if begging for something.

Sea otters also cough and sneeze. Perhaps they aren't feeling well. They also yawn. Could they be tired? Or bored?

When they are really scared, two otters may fling their arms around each other and hold on tight.

A Sea Otter Pup Is Born

Sea otters show all sorts of feelings. But almost everyone agrees that the strongest emotion in the otter world is love — the love of a mother for her pup.

Male and female otters usually stay in separate rafts. But when it is time to mate, a male and female swim off together. For three or four days they eat and sleep and play only with each other. Often they can be heard making soft *ku-ku-kuing* sounds to each other. It's their way of saying, "I like you." But then they seem to lose interest. Each goes off to its own raft again. From now on the job of raising the pup will belong to the female alone.

The beginning of life for a southern sea otter is a mystery. Is a pup born head first like a walrus? Or tail first like a whale? Nobody knows — for southern sea otter pups are born at sea, and no one has ever seen the exact moment of birth.

One thing is certain — the mother otter gives birth to only one baby at a time. She could not take care of a larger family in her wet and often cold and stormy world.

As soon as the pup is born the mother scoops it out of the water and puts it on her chest. Now the little one begins to cry for food, just like any hungry human baby. But the mother pays no attention. She knows she has a job to do first.

A newborn sea otter pup is covered with a coat of yellow-brown fur. This coat is rough and thick and looks like wool. That's why many people call very young otters "woolly pups." The coat is also sopping wet. So before the newborn can be allowed to do anything else it must be groomed — or it would quickly freeze to death.

The mother licks its head and back and belly. She licks its two floppy flippers and stringy little tail. Her sharp claws comb through its fur. She even blow-dries the soft hairs behind the pup's ears.

All the while the pup wails in its high, sharp baby voice. It doesn't like all this rough pulling and tugging and rubbing and scrubbing.

But the mother just continues to comb and lick and blow until every inch of her pup's coat is as fluffy and dry and full of warm air as her own. Only then will she turn her pup around and guide it to one of her nipples for its first meal of rich otter milk.

The pup is born in water, yet it can't swim. But sometimes a mother has to go off and feed herself. She has to leave her pup behind. This could be a very dangerous time for the young otter. True, it's wrapped in a blanket of air, so it can float. But what if it drifted out to sea? Or a sudden wave swept it onto the sharp rocks by the shore?

The mother otter makes sure this doesn't happen. She swims to a nearby patch of kelp and puts her pup down on top of some of the long, thin strands of seaweed. Then she rolls the pup over and over like a ball. The stringy strands wrap all around it. Now she can go off without worrying. She knows her young one will be safe until she returns to untangle it — cradled it in its bed of kelp.

Lessons to Learn

At first a pup's whole world is its mother's chest. But when a sea otter is about two weeks old it's time for swimming lessons to begin. The mother otter simply sinks beneath her baby and swims a little distance away. She begins to make soft, coaxing sounds. "There's nothing to be afraid of," the sounds seem to say.

The little one doesn't agree. It thrashes and splashes in place, crying as loudly as it can. "Help! Come back!" it is answering just as clearly.

The mother pays no attention. She just continues to make the same coaxing sounds. And finally the little one begins to move its hind flippers up and down. It doesn't know it, but it is taking its first awkward strokes.

The first day the pup only manages to swim a few inches before it gets tired. But day by day the pup grows stronger. Soon it will be completely at home in the water, swimming on both its back and its stomach.

Swimming is just the first lesson a growing otter must learn. Next the little sea animal must master the skill of diving. This is a very important lesson, for most of the food it will one day eat is to be found on the ocean floor far below.

How does the little otter learn this skill? By watching. For weeks it has seen its mother slip down into the mysterious depths. *Where is she going? Why can't I go, too?* it must be feeling.

Finally the young otter can stand it no longer and tries to follow. But it cannot. It manages to get its head under water, but that's all. The rest of its air-filled body just bobs about like a cork. Its hind flippers paddle helplessly in the empty air.

Time passes and the pup gets stronger. By the time the otter is two months old it is able to make its first shallow dive.

Its troubles are still not over. The first few times the pup finds itself under the surface it shoots right back up to the top again, sputtering and spitting out water. For there is another lesson the pup must learn — how to hold its breath underwater.

Young otters usually master this skill while playing with their friends. The kelp beds make wonderful underwater playgrounds. The growing otters spend hours each day darting through the forest of kelp stems, playing endless otter games. As they do, they are learning to hold their breaths for longer and longer periods without coming up for a fresh gulp of air. Finally they are able to hold their breaths for as long as their mothers can — about four minutes or so.

Even when a young otter can dive all the way to the bottom, it still doesn't know what to eat. At first it treats anything it finds there as a toy. The young otter watches its mother carry things up to the surface to eat. So it carries things up, too — but more often than not they are pebbles or empty clam shells. So this, too, is something to learn — what and how to eat.

At first a mother takes away any food her very young pup may pick up. Milk is the only thing she allows it to swallow at first. But by the time the pup is two or three months old she begins trying to interest it in solid food.

One day she puts a piece of food — perhaps it is a chunk of crab — on its chest. The young otter picks it up . . . sniffs at it . . . then lets it fall into the water.

The next day the mother tries again. Once more she puts a piece of crab on her little one's chest. Once more the young otter picks it up . . . sniffs at it . . . and this time nibbles a little off one side.

In a few days crab will surely be part of its menu. So a bit of this and a bit of that — that's how a growing otter learns to know all the different good things to eat.

Sea otters must also learn to groom their own coats. By the time a pup is six months old it's doing most of the work by itself. But it still counts on its mother to help with the hard-to-reach places.

Growing Up

Newborn otters usually lie quietly on their mothers' chests. But medium-sized pups are much more restless. Sometimes they tumble about, playing some private game. They turn and twist in all directions. But if they become too rough, the mother just dumps them into the water. She has found it's a very good way to say, "That's enough!"

By the time an otter is eight months old it is able to take care of itself. Now it spends more and more time with other young otters. But when it is lonely or very tired it swims right back to its mother again.

The mother doesn't seem to mind. But one day she senses that it is time to say good-bye. Now she just slips away to another raft. If her child is a female it may end up in the same raft. If it is a male it will swim around until it finds a raft of males to join. Either way, the young otter will live on its own from now on.

Nobody knows just how long a sea otter lives. Otter experts think that the otter's life span is somewhere between 15 and 20 years.

Even when it is almost full-grown, an otter pup may sometimes climb on its mother's chest as it did when it was small. The mother seems to understand.

The Most Dangerous Enemy of All

There's one thing a mother otter doesn't have to teach her pup — what to be afraid of in the sea. Sea otters have no natural enemies. Other sea mammals must be alert at all times. Sharks are their enemies. So are killer whales. But sea otters don't have to worry about these hungry hunters.

Usually killer whales and sharks swim right by a raft of sea otters and don't even turn their heads. Why aren't they interested in these littlest of sea mammals? Scientists aren't sure, but they think one reason is that the otter does not have blubber. All the other mammals of the sea have a fatty layer of blubber under their skins. Killer whales and sharks are probably very fond of that fat. So sea otters just don't taste greasy enough for them.

Scientists think otters may be safe for another reason — their fine fur coats. They think that every once in a while a killer whale or shark may try to attack a sea otter. But they quickly lose interest, because their teeth become tangled in the otter's thick fur.

A sea otter's furry coat may keep it safe today. But for many, many years that rich fur meant just the opposite — almost certain death.

For hundreds of years sea otters had an enemy far more deadly than any killer whale or shark — man.

A coat made of otter fur is soft and warm and thick. It lasts a long time. Most important, it is very good-looking. Many people say it is the most beautiful fur in the world.

Once, millions of sea otters lived off many different coasts. But in the early 1700s the hunting began. The ships of many nations sailed the seas, looking for sea otters to kill.

For years everyone was happy — the people who killed otters and the people who bought their pelts. In Japan, rich lords and ladies refused to wear any other fur. Only otter-skin robes and gowns and hats and belts were good enough for them.

But eventually the hunters became too greedy. They killed so many otters that it was difficult to find any at all. By the early 1900s, otter skins were so rare that a single one sold for more than a thousand dollars. And each year there were fewer to be found.

Finally in 1911 something was done. A group of people called *conservationists* — men and women who work to save all living things — came to the sea otter's aid. They got the governments of most of the big nations who hunted otters to sign a treaty. This agreement between nations said that from now on it was against the law to kill sea otters.

But what good could this law do? For it seemed that there were no more otters left to kill. The hunters had done their work too well. They had wiped out a whole species.

Then one day in 1938, a man and his wife happened to be walking along the California coast. They looked out to sea and noticed a small group of plump, brown animals in the water.

Some were just resting, belly up. Others were diving and eating and playing. One was busy nursing a pup.

The couple called a game warden at a nearby state park. And before the day was over the good news had begun to spread. The sea otters had come back!

Somehow a few otters had managed to survive in wild and secret places. Slowly they had multiplied. Since that day of discovery in the 1930s, the population continued to grow for many years.

Today sea otters are protected by man-made laws. But it is an uneasy friendship. There are only about 1,300 southern sea otters off the coast of California, and every year they face more man-made dangers.

Fishermen's nets are a big problem for sea otters. Often the nets that are meant to trap fish trap the otters as well. And before they can break free, they drown.

Another problem is the chemicals that are used to spray nearby fruit and vegetable farms. Often rain washes these dangerous pesticides into the sea — poisoning the water.

Sometimes factories spill other chemicals into the ocean. Passing ships dump oil. And waste from sewage plants pollutes the water.

With all this, sea otters often have a hard time keeping clean. They must groom harder than ever to keep their coats from matting and clumping. Remember, it's a matter of life and death.

Sea Otters and People

Sea otters are wild animals. So they usually move away if a swimmer or a boat tries to get too close. But they are also full of curiosity about everything that is happening around them.

Once some filmmakers were working from a boat. One warm day a young member of the crew named Phillipe decided to take a swim. He dived into the water and paddled around for a while. Suddenly he realized he wasn't alone. Paddling nearby was a furry sea otter.

The man and the wild animal stared at each other for a moment. Then quickly Phillipe rolled over on his back — that favorite of all otter positions — and signaled to the boat for something to eat.

Someone threw him a cooked crab. The otter eyed him for a moment more and then held out a paw. It was a clear invitation: "Please give me some, too."

So Phillipe broke off a chunk of crab and handed it to the otter. For the next few minutes the new friends floated along side by side — happily munching a lunch of crab.

Other wild otters have made friends with people. But most are not nearly so bold. So people who wanted to know more about sea otters began to capture them and put them in *oceanariums*.

An oceanarium is really a bit of man-made ocean on dry land. It's a place where everyone can come and see all sorts of sea creatures living naturally in big salt-water pools.

Now for the first time people could really study sea otters up close. And they learned many interesting things.

The first was that sea otters become tame very quickly. Often an otter will take food from a human hand on its very first day in the pool. Just a few days later it will swim to the side of the pool, climb out, stand on its hind legs, and beg when its dinner arrives.

Another thing otter-watchers soon learned is that these ocean-going animals have strong likes and dislikes. Some people they go to right away. Others they never warm up to.

People also learned that sea otters are not all alike. Some are outgoing and full of high spirits. Others are very shy and serious. Some are very bright. Others have a hard time learning new things. Some just want to be left alone, and others are willing to make friends with almost anyone.

And by watching sea otters in captivity we now know a lot about what they like to eat. There's no doubt about it, a favorite food is abalone. Otters are also especially fond of octopus and sea urchins and clams. Depending on how hungry they are, they will eat many other foods. But if you feed them the same food for too long they may turn up their noses and swim away.

People have learned many things by watching sea otters in oceanariums. But not many oceanariums house sea otters today.

Sea otters are very sensitive animals. They don't always thrive in a man-made sea. They get sick or even die. Only rarely are baby otters born in captivity. And even healthy pups often don't live very long.

So sea otters are still best seen where they live so happily and well — eating and playing and swimming and sleeping in the salty sea.

But it's not always easy to spot a sea otter, even on a calm, clear day. For remember, sea otters spend most of their time near beds of giant seaweed. And their shiny brown coats blend in all too well with the brownish-green strands of kelp.

Otter-watchers know some signs that help them spot the otters — even in the middle of a patch of kelp.

- They watch the surface of the water for the ripples a sea otter makes as it swims along.
- They look for seagulls hovering over the water. The birds are waiting to snatch bits of food the sea otter drops while it is eating.
- They listen for the shrill, high sound of a baby otter — crying for its mother or its next meal.
- And they listen for the *rat-a-tat-tat* sound of shells being pounded against the sea otter's special tool — the rock.

If you follow these suggestions, you, too, may see a group of sea otters one day. Good luck!

The Family to the North

This book is about southern sea otters. But another group of ocean-going otters — called northern sea otters — lives off the coast of Alaska.

Both groups belong to the same family, and they are so much alike that it is impossible to tell them apart just by looking. But there are differences between them all the same.

One difference is size. Northern sea otters are larger. The largest southern sea otter ever weighed was 87 pounds. The largest northern otter tipped the scales at 102 — a full 15 pounds more.

California otters usually search for food in water not much deeper than 50 feet. But the Alaskan otters dive deeper. They are often found diving to 180 feet. And one was seen at the surface of water 318 feet deep with a bottom-dwelling crab in its mouth.

There are more northern sea otters — over 100,000 make their homes off the coast of Alaska. There are only 1,200 to 1,300 adult southern otters in California waters.

Their food is somewhat different, too. Southern sea otters almost never eat fish. Fish makes up about half of a northern sea otter's diet.

The use of a tool seems to belong to the southern sea otter alone. A wild northern otter has never been seen to crack open anything with a stone.

And otter-watchers are always surprised when they see a southern sea otter on a rock or a beach. They know that these otters almost never leave their watery home. But northern otters often haul out to sunbathe or sleep in some protected cove. And females come ashore to give birth — something no southern sea otter mother-to-be has ever been seen to do.

Margaret Davidson has written other books about animals.
Here are some you may want to read:

Dolphins!

Nine True Dolphin Stories

Wild Animal Families

Five True Dog Stories

Five True Horse Stories